CHROMA

CHROMA

FIVE CENTURIES OF WOMEN ARTISTS

poems by

SHARON TRACEY

Shanti Arts Publishing
Brunswick, Maine

CHROMA
Five Centuries of Women Artists

Published by Shanti Arts Publishing
Interior and cover design by Shanti Arts Designs

Cover images: [top left] Paula Modersohn-Becker, *Self-Portrait on the Sixth Wedding Anniversary,* 1906. Tempera on canvas. 40 x 27.6 inches (101.8 x 70.2 cm). Paula Modersohn-Becker Museum, Bremen, Germany. [top right] Marie Bashkirtseff, The Umbrella, 1883. Oil on canvas. 36.6 x 29.1 inches (93 x 74 cm). The State Russian Museum, Saint Petersburg, Russia. [bottom left] Anna Ancher, *The Maid in the Kitchen,* 1883–6. Oil on canvas. 26.9 x 34.5 inches (68.5 x 87.7 cm). The Hirschsprung Collection, Copenhagen, Denmark. [bottom right] Helene Schjerfbeck, *Self-Portrait with Black Background,* 1915. Oil on canvas. 17.9 x 14.2 inches (45.5 x 36 cm). Finnish National Gallery, Helsinki, Finland. All images are in the public domain and are available on Wikimedia Commons.

Shanti Arts LLC
193 Hillside Road
Brunswick, Maine 04011
shantiarts.com

Printed in the United States of America

ISBN: 978-1-951651-49-7 (softcover)

Library of Congress Control Number: 2020946675

for my family

You may forget but
Let me tell you
this: someone in
some future time
will think of us

—Sappho

Painting is silent poetry,
and poetry is painting that speaks.

—Simonides of Ceos

Contents

The Opening: Fourteen Ways of Looking at a Painting ... 13

Gallery I: Paintings 2013 – 1984

Horizon Bird ... 19
Empirical Construction, Istanbul ... 20
Branching A ... 21
Morning Glory ... 22
Ocean ... 23
Waterfall ... 24
Air: 24 Hours, Five P.M. ... 25
Dormant Grass #6 ... 26
Miss Everything (Unsuppressed Deliverance) ... 27
The Other Side—Betty Ford, Six of Hearts ... 28
Mount Tamalpais ... 29
Box of Coloured Objects ... 30
Night Flying In ... 31

Gallery II: Paintings 1973 – 1940

Cherry Blossom Symphony ... 35
Green and White ... 36
Summer ... 37
On Me Fait Signe ... 38
Girls in the Surf with Moon Casting a Shadow ... 39
Cementerio ... 40
Milkweed ... 41
Rutu ... 42
Olive Plantation ... 43
Fishes ... 44
Self-Portrait with Thorn Necklace and Hummingbird ... 45
I Have No Shadow ... 46

Gallery III: Paintings 1938 – 1883

Star Gazing in Texas ... 51
Microcosm and Macrocosm ... 52

Un Mundo 53
Postcard 54
Morning 55
Self-Portrait with Black Background 56
Electric Prisms 57
The Fortune Teller 58
Self-Portrait on the Sixth Wedding Anniversary 59
Sita and Sarita 60
The Maid in the Kitchen 61
The Umbrella 62
Sunshine in the Blue Room 63

Gallery IV: Paintings 1878 – 1559

Moonlight, study 67
A Nun 68
Ploughing in the Nivernais 69
Self-Portrait Hesitating between Music and Painting 70
Self-Portrait 71
Metamorphosis 72
Flowers in a Glass Vase 73
Still Life of Flowers 74
The Triumph of Bacchus 75
Judith Slaying Holofernes 76
Noli Me Tangere 77
Bernandino Campi Painting Sofonisba Anguissola 78

The Closing: Fourteen Paintings by Mary Frank 81

Artists 83
Notes 85
Acknowledgments 87
About the Author 89

The Opening

Fourteen Ways of Looking at a Painting

1
Among seven rising seas
the only still thing
was the eye of the painting.

2
I was of four minds
like the seasons
which are always changing.

3
The painting spoke in prism tongues.
It was the voice of a woman.

4
A woman and a man are one
and not the same. A woman
and another woman and a painting
are one and not the same.

5
I do not know which to love more—
the poetry of the painting
or its chroma,
the painting's lament
or its echo.

6
Waves filled the house
with kelp and shells.
The composition of the painting
was wet
in the making.
Not yet
a recognizable face.

7
O dear poets, why do you imagine
blackbirds? The painting harbors
an unborn child, an amber necklace.
Can you not see the artist
is the mother?

8
I know birth is no accident
and fate a fickle inescapable fact
but I do not know
how the painting could not be involved
in what I know.

9
When the painting was born
she looked to the sky and inside
herself. Then chose a name.

10
She carried the painting
into the light
where the old masters paused
to look and listen to its cry.

11
The woman rowed a wooden boat
across the centuries.
Once, a fear pierced her,
in that she mistook
the darkness
for the end of the painting.

12
The climate changed and strong currents
pushed the woman and the painting.

13
It was the seventh day
all evening. The wind
blew backwards
through time,
unraveling.

14
The woman and the painting
could see a distant shore
an opening—

Gallery I

Paintings 2013 - 1984

Horizon Bird

Mary Frank · 2012 · oil and acrylic on panel

Attached to her chest, she paints what appears—

a pine branch blocked in burning ice
that the sun will eventually melt, but maybe

she wants what light does right now, wants
to pray at a pyre for what's left in the world.

She's flower-pressed specimens on the vanes
of her feathered vest—tattooed shells, pollen

spores, a moraine left in the wake
of a glacier—stand-ins for all of nature.

Beneath her, the earth lies dusted

as a cinnamon moon, punctuated
with rogue rocks that might be tombstones.

She's a wading bird without a wetland, a great egret
splitting the salmon sky with her long neck as if

a pair of lungs or hanging breasts—
the way so many things appear to be another.

At sunrise, I stand at the kitchen window
and look north across the field to the far edge

a line of blackbirds descending—

set my eyes upon a row of white pines
cut like cuspid teeth against the pink sky

waiting—to become another thing.

Empirical Construction, Istanbul

Julie Mehretu · 2003 · acrylic and ink on canvas

The way a city gathers memories, another
atmosphere, flags fluttering, reels of clothesline,
sirens, flower sellers, crowds dispersing like confetti—

what is built is built from bits, blueprints
of future plans—scaffolding for mosque and church,
housing for newlyweds, strangers, and soldiers

the narrative is what you make it—

In an old photograph, I'm the Catholic girl
on her honeymoon in Istanbul, late
afternoon, wearing my new husband's old sweater

standing near the Blue Mosque with a forest green
bag and a loaf of bread, the sky slowly filling
with sonorous calls to evening prayer—

so many different things capable of proof,
the way they're put together
clay to brick, dome to minaret, the unsung labor

someone sees—

On the Bosphorus, a string of boats chugs north,
outdoor cafés clink glass as waiters pass
trays of Turkish coffee

beneath us—
two continents collide in the dark.

Branching A

Emmi Whitehorse · 2009 · oil and chalk on paper mounted on canvas

There were many reasons to stop.
Paper-flat fields, pearled, the sun stuck
like silver duct tape to distant hills,
white moths sputtering like first snowflakes,
the dance of the Greater Sage-Grouse
we hoped to see. We were hungry.

We rambled for weeks on empty roads,
past mesas, slot canyons, tumbleweed
caught in the crooks of trees.
Who could argue with Navajo
philosophy: *beauty nature harmony.*
Land of the mountain bluebird,
elf owl, road runner. Four Corners.

Floating marks and flint of desert rock,
sagebrush and saltbush, gold tones
diffusing light. Marks that prick memory.
Maybe because of drought and dust
the wish for water not surprising.
For a split second I thought of
Klee but quickly stepped back:

this land is hers. Every arc, petroglyph,
imagined bloom of greenthread, each
shape and line expressed as birthmark.
Hands that press the grounds, walk
the dry washes. The cottonwoods I
remember, the hidden roots branching
into ever smaller roots like alveoli
in a desert lung. A single morning stung
with rare rain, the water iron red.

Morning Glory

Astrid Preston · 2007 · oil on canvas

For her I washed the clothes,
I chose a ribbon.
I listened—
silence was its own
white noise, weft of gauze,
inexplicable as heard.

For her I placed a tooth
under a pillow,
made a wish—
a quartered-counter-sound
absorbent and reduced
like a fine sauce
so as not to wake her.

The world didn't start
this way. I didn't see
myself, that I could split
in two and return
another day.

For her I paused—
I swooned.
I slid into motherhood
like a tender seedling
in the spring garden

pushing particles
of soil aside, sliding
towards sunlight
into something not sought
but once arrived—

I was the vine,
she was
the morning glory.

Ocean

Vija Celmins · 1990 · oil on canvas

she looks
at ocean
close-up
crests of waves

droplets pressed
redescriptions
she calls them

I call them
soul portals
mind motion

she calls some
Untitled

she says, it takes
just a second

for knowledge
to go—*bam*
all the way in

then you are
there—

no horizon
no scale
but something
small, smaller

feels more
infinite
more intimate—
an opening

Waterfall

April Gornik • 1995 • oil on linen

If at a certain point
over the course of
it may come when
the river leaves you
when it crosses
where you erode
where it cliff-bends
a rapids descent
the body cut—
cataracts cascading
streaming viscous, this
lithological myth-maker,
stone-creaser—
how it echoes, flows,
how it laments, foments
how we change
looking back—
the cadence easing
until you no longer
hear the rushing—
the gold light standing in
for the sound
as it splits the darkest rock
and leaves its recording
the light standing in
for the sound

AIR: 24 HOURS, FIVE P.M.

Jennifer Bartlett · 1991–92 · oil on canvas

How do you build a painting with only
sixty minutes to live
between five and six in the evening
on a seven square-foot grid—

she's dug a fishpond in a courtyard
fissured it in time
stocked it with cold-blooded koi
dressed in calico and straw yellow

some seem dredged in flour as if
they might be battered

they dart among the water lilies
then tip their scales and slip
under as if cold war spies—

some limp leaves float
on the placid surface
like Matisse cutouts that have died.

So much happens in a single hour
and so little—you stare
at the appearance of depth
and think of the fish, the ticking clock,
where the weeping light goes

realize you could just walk away
just take something and walk—

Dormant Grass #6

Karen Kitchel · 2009 · oil on birch panel

Something as simple as the fact of grass—
its soft comfort, its effort
across savanna,
steppe and prairie   the lonely
sprouts on railroad tracks

tilling the earth, the grass goes on—

Its sheaf I use to sweep the house.

We eat when hungry.   Wait
for whom we serve   longing
not knowing who will come.

Wind blows the pedicels,
the small stalked feet
who bear the inflorescence
of inconspicuous flowers.

I dream.

Endless waves in multitudes,
the shapes I love:
ligulate, spikelet, awn.

On the kitchen wall I hang
the sheath and blade.

Miss Everything (Unsuppressed Deliverance)

Amy Sherald · 2013 · oil on canvas

Dear Ms. Sherald,

I was first introduced to you through the work—
Miss Everything (Unsuppressed Deliverance)—winner
of the National Portrait Gallery's 2016 Outwin
Boochever Portrait Competition. Giant white cup
and saucer, formal white gloves, her frank expression.
Her dress half polka-dotted and half black, from a vintage
store in Baltimore, the crimson hat you saved for the right
occasion, eyes that show the worth of looking. Skin
painted gray as a seal and made with your signature
mix—Naples yellow and black.

I stood before her, both moved and still, drawn
in by how *Miss Everything* occupies the space, stands
her ground and confronts the viewer. How you devise
and paint the guise: calm and relational. Regal in stature
in the garments you have carefully chosen to be
worn, to be shouldered.

A beautiful melancholy—neutral but not—
instills and leaves uncertainty, something that clings
like static, feels that electric. That rinses like a sheet
of glass, becoming both window and mirror.
Somewhere, between mistakes and accidents of birth
and history, you pinpoint a clarity. Pose questions
and provoke answers as if you are canvassing us.
Can acceptance ever equal forgiveness? Or to cut
more to the point—what does it mean to be free?

Sincerely,

This Viewer / A Fan

The Other Side—Betty Ford, Six of Hearts

Tina Mion · 1999 · oil on three linens

Years ago, on a family trip out West,
finding ourselves in Winslow, Arizona
we splurged and checked into La Posada,
Mary Colter's 1930 hacienda masterpiece
restored by Tina Mion and her husband.

That afternoon, we seemed to have the place
to ourselves except for Spunky, the blind basset
hound who slept on cool tiles in the lobby,
and Mion's paintings of First Ladies hanging
on the public walls. The one I loved best—

Betty Ford in a brick red dress, leaning, almost
leaving the left side of the triptych, her right
hand raised as if caught in the middle of
a dance move as Gerald enters the canvas
stage right, unseen by Betty.

In front of the center panel, our children
play a game of chess, as if they are part of
the painting, positioned between Betty's
outstretched left arm and a six of hearts
playing card. I still have the photo. I knew

the First Lady was a cancer survivor and advocate
but I didn't know she was a dancer who trained
with Martha Graham. The artist gets to choose
the story. The painting takes the stage. Sometimes
you find yourself inside, can hold the heart.

Mount Tamalpais

Etel Adnan • 1985 • oil on canvas

Breeze had come all the way
from Athens and Baghdad,

to the Bay,
led me to Mountain

most important person ever met.

Geographic spot becomes spiritual,
I watch its colors.

Community sleeps at its feet
hidden by steam

the world has the darkness.

Mountain remains blue
purple desertion nobody knows.

Do not climb
unless you know
it needs you

carry your skeleton,
trees healing.

Everything upside down.

Mountain appears
like an Angel
chasing clouds in circles.

—from *Journey to Mount Tamalpais* by Etel Adnan

Box of Coloured Objects

Lucy Mackenzie · 2010 · oil on board · plus sixteen more paintings by the artist

Two shuttlecocks. Flower in a lustre cup. Ball of string. Yellow cup and china dog. Fragile box with scissors. Strawberry and glass. Striped cup and paper bag. Toy truck on a printed cloth. Pewter pot and pearls. Three shells and a feather. Pear and fork. Vermeer eyes with pearls. Leonardo lady with torn paper. Yellow tulip, black bowl. Three observer's books. Modern art.

Night Flying In

Helen Lundeburg • 1984 • acrylic on canvas • plus fifteen more paintings by the artist

All the angles.
Streetlight in shadows.

Double-portrait of the artist in time.
Biological fantasy.

Light path to the sea.
A quiet place. Winter sun. White trees.

Seen from a height—

Oracle.
Great cloud.
Two mountains.
Sundown shadow.
Tidelands.
The poet's road.

Gallery II

Paintings 1973 – 1940

Cherry Blossom Symphony

Alma Thomas · 1973 · acrylic on canvas

I walked to the brick row house
where Alma Thomas lived for 70 years
on 15th Street in Washington D.C.

A man stood with his green hose
watering the shadows of her flowers,
says, *I've been inside, seen the studio*

the kitchen corner where she turned
the natural world into chips of light,
painted the world as it might be—

Scarlet Sage Dancing a Whirling Dervish.
Wind and Crepe Myrtle Concerto.
March on Washington.
Resurrection.

I stood in the April sun talking to Dave
as he watered, the cherry blossoms bursting
as they dropped petals like pink confetti

and remembered her words: *Through color,*
I have sought to concentrate on beauty and happiness,
rather than on man's inhumanity to man.

Thought, we have come too far to walk away.

Green and White

Sandra Blow • 1969 • acrylic, ash and charcoal on canvas

Maybe she means to say something
about stripping away, about waiting

for liberation on any brilliant corner
more exposure, more eroding

whiplashed by wind, the shearing of
a face. How far might we be moved

to change? Each corner in a different
hue—sap, pea, moss, malachite—

patched as plots of grass. Beyond stretch
bandaged roads, strips of salt-chalk-ash.

I have walked in space like this—

slabs of sidewalk, unmarked miles along
a road, no sign for where to turn or how

to choose—the world sun-bleached,
the greenest greens growing slow—

maybe all of this means nothing or maybe
it's what Blake says, *a world in a grain of sand.*

Summer

Agnes Martin · 1964 · watercolor, ink and gouache on paper

as if a square of sky could grid a life
the shimmer
of some faded afternoon
that might at any time

be amplified or silenced

a drop of rain
a swimmer's stroke,
the mind afloat

she gathers all of summer
in the air
and drops the days
into her humble squares
to warble there
like water

so I can see how being born
on the vast plains
of Saskatchewan

where it can seem
to take days for a train
to come and slowly pass
through
to its vanishing point

might make you blue or help you
see what lasts,
what goes—

On Me Fait Signe

Natalia Dumitrescu • 1964 • oil on canvas

Notes to self upon entering
a painting: come look, let
something go—Push
into a tangle
of color—

Be brave. Sign up.

Let lines and shapes speak:
make a street, a scrim,
a promise. A patch
of blue, a rub of sorrel.

Not scripture set in stone, not
earmarked walls or boundaries,
but geometries that give you height,
a sense of flight across a country.

What language it is I don't know
but I love to read it.

As if from a plane cutting through clouds—
blocks of states interlocking
then breaking apart
not knowing—
what will come.

Girls in the Surf with Moon Casting a Shadow

Joan Brown · 1962 · oil on canvas

Alcatraz swim
sourdough sky

to crawl like that
kicking and breathing

dripping darts
in San Francisco Bay

day after day
cold-cold currents

slippery as a newborn baby

the Golden Gate Bridge
spanning space—

ferry, freighter,
rose silhouette

hip of island
prison above

the waves glissade.

Phosphorus moon
in shadow and glow

casting spells
between two worlds

painted by surf
how girls emerge.

Cementerio

Tilsa Tsuchiya · 1958 · oil on canvas

two in indigo are mourning
the mood
like Picasso's Blue Period

but this all hers in Peru
more electric blue, more neon

hunched near a crypt
five stark crosses
the ground a carmine carpet

where are we anyway
when someone dies

who is the woman, who is the man?

maybe she is *Pachamama*
the Great Earth Mother
pockets full
of sacred Wak'as rocks

maybe he is an old bird
with a broken wing
head hidden by a blue claw
except for one
exposed eye
still as a black egg in a nest

her paintings send messengers

Milkweed

Lee Krasner · 1955 · oil, paper, and canvas collage on canvas

From the modest upstairs bedroom
she used as her studio in Springs,
the field spreads itself, sloping
gently to the water's fringed edge—

imagine taking blade to old canvases,
cutting and ripping off strips
of paintings deemed not good enough,
freeing them to collage in another.

I see a field—black clouds of roses,
black habits of nuns, torn ribs, fat lips,
sheaths of leaves, a rumble of thunder.
Pods split open to spit out clouds

of seed, another chance to reassemble
a mixed-up world, to extract something.
Field as key, a guide brought to life
by the overgrown summer. I'm reminded

of the story I heard—how as a young artist
she nailed mirrors to the trees to paint herself
one summer. And I wonder if the orange
slash might be a glimpse of monarch wing, or else

the sharper thing—a shard of girl.

Rutu

Rita Angus · 1951 · oil on canvas

As Ruth gleaned barley in the fields, maybe you
fished the Tasman Sea, coaxed those minnows
onto the collar of your blood-red jersey,
you made blonde with chocolate skin
in this self-portrait: half-white and half-Maori.
Imagining yourself an indigenous goddess
who dares to wear the sun as a halo.
But if hands are roots, why barely touch
the sacred lotus which seems to grow out
of you, stamen and stigma hidden, the torus
torn between two in a mixed marriage.
Maybe someday, someone will look
out the window and finally see
a woman who can walk on water.

Olive Plantation

Dorrit Black · 1946 · oil on canvas

The olive trees hold hidden leaves
carved like clay, arranged
in curvaceous, voluptuous rows
woven over
rolling hills like a knobby blanket.

From a distance—

shaped like so many bread loaves,
pats of rising dough are dabbed
in moss, pickle, pear, and sage

so now I'm hungry

the brushstrokes pared
to simple needs
this most drupaceous fruit
offering up its essence,
these trees so loved by gods
as a sign of peace and prosperity.

Sky runs a turquoise finger
across the upper ledge of canvas
—squeezed in—
but not claustrophobic

one tower of cloud
rising above
the foothills near Magill—

you can dip your fingers in.

Fishes

Amelia Peláez • 1943 • oil on canvas

When she passed the pescado and circled back
for the four of them
what was floating through her mind

why did she decide to paint them like stained glass—
fire red, yarrow yellow, hornet green—
splayed overlapping on the serving plate

startled eyes filling holes and all that black
crowded with *criollo,* the iron wrought
the table clothed, the balustrade baroque—

where did she learn to cut patterns for a cubist cloth
ornamental as an ornament of love, instrumental
as an instrument of need, so lavishly adorned—

Somewhere in Havana there is a house,
inside the house lives a woman
inside the woman
a bird
within its beak—
a map

Self-Portrait with Thorn Necklace and Hummingbird

Frida Kahlo • 1940 • oil on canvas

Frida Kahlo, ex-voto headdress goddess
of the butterfly clips, dragonflies and lush
insects, leaves the body out of it, gives us

her head, solemn gaze, a twisted braid. A bust,
nothing lower. Paints a panther, a monkey
behind her shoulders. No one wants to be cliché,

locked in a precious box. Hummingbird,
a good luck charm for falling in love, here
it's dead, a pendant hanging from choker

of briar and thorn. Who wants to be martyr,
wear the crown? If you follow the backstory,
the naming of parts—scapula, spine, pelvis—

it still won't tell the whole truth, what sets
the spark. Where shall we find the skull, clavicle,
corsets, the thirty-two operations? What is lived

cannot be broken from a woman's work. *Soma*—
the body as tomb an ancient thought. Still, we
breathe, we bleed. Put pretty pins in our hair.

I Have No Shadow

Kay Sage · 1940 · oil on canvas

She says she has no shadow
but she is a shaman of shadows
she paints two stone cliffs   the rift
you can barely see a couple   in the middle
distance   a confined existence

I want to know what substance
creates shadows
with hidden stairs
that lead   to doors
a shallow shell
darkness that might   open
to others

Sage paintings have questions for you—

some type of scaffolding   surreal
and somewhat sinister
what you may find   or not
or read or not   between the lines
think that
the act   is
planned
won't see it   coming

two bullets shot through the canvas : *Watching the Clock*

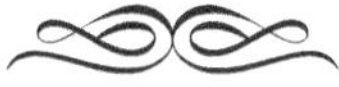

Gallery III

Paintings 1938 – 1883

Star Gazing in Texas

Ida Ten Eyck O'Keeffe · 1938 · oil on canvas

Whittier, California, 1961

To whomever finds this letter,

Yes, I am the younger sister, two years younger.
I died twenty-five years before Georgia—the two of us
long estranged. Both our grandmothers were painters
and I'm the one with an MFA from Columbia. You
probably will not recognize my name or know
that my celebrated sister had sisters. Or that Stieglitz,
her famous husband, flirted and tried to lure me
with romantic letters. That I never took the bait.
The Depression was a struggle. With no dealer
to champion my work, I moved across the country,
teaching. Contemplating the meaning of art.
Who gets to make it? Who decides what counts?
And always gnawing at me—under what circumstances
is blood thicker than water?
Many of my paintings have an underlying geometry,
an abstract quality, but this one, *Star Gazing in Texas*,
is a narrative and a favorite, painted when I taught
in San Antonio. There is nothing like star gazing
in a spacious place when the world feels boxed in
and in danger of imploding.
Now I find myself in these final years reminiscing
far from my start in Sun Prairie. In a room full of finished
paintings, waiting. I cannot see the future—nor the curator
who will notice my signature on a painting many years
from now, who will search for more work. What is a legacy
made of. Who might open the door and return a missing
part of ourselves? The hand that holds my brushes aches,
my eyes are filled with stars.

Sincerely,

Ida Ten Eyck O'Keeffe

Microcosm and Macrocosm

Helen Lundeberg · 1937 · oil on Masonite

the shoreline was where it began
the sky and sea traded faces
a refreshment or a terror
to be suspended uncertain
which is up which is down
air and water mixing not like oil
swimming in a pool of plankton
ringed by planet sea of speckled stars
amoeba creatures drinking air and water

she's a giant fragment looming
on the left ledge long edge
looking through a lens
finger to temple mind to microbe
how small things magnify the largest

if you were lying underwater
almost lost a daughter the universe so wide
lungs could not hold breath the longest
if someone called you to the surface
would you be saved?

Un Mundo

Ángeles Santos · 1929 · oil on canvas

tell me where they end, the stars
    that fire from the sun
who chars the world,
    makes corners
for its turning—

in a Spanish town
    there was an angel painting
a child of nineteen, some say
    the Spanish Rimbaud—

she held a vision of a hanging world—

with wisps of women climbing stairs
    to light the stars they carried
and all of time was there in violet scarves—

whispering the words of Jiménez that moved her as a child—
    vague mauve angels
    were putting out the green stars

what happens when you reach a peak so early?

meet moon-faced women making music for a lifetime,
    have seen the strings that web the stars—

Postcard

Tarsila do Amaral · 1928 · oil on canvas · plus ten more paintings by the artist

Dear Viewer,

São Paulo. cityscape.
hillside shanty towns.
angels.
the bull.
the moon. the egg.
the lake. the forest.

I learn and step.

xoxo
Tarsila

Morning

Dod Procter • 1926 • oil on canvas

Dod Procter brought Cissie Barnes
to this room—smoothed the sheets
with a palette knife, the model reclining

on her left side, sheathed in a modest slip
her ankles crossed, knees snugly pressed,
all sixteen years caressed by sleep

pillows plumped, the shadows arrested
on the bedsheets as if bruised fruit,
pale yellow and purple-cornered.

Some will call the painting modern,
the girl's future we don't know
but maybe it's enough to be in love

with the triangles inside her elbows
how the violet shadows stroke
the V-neck on her chest.

Self-Portrait with Black Background

Helene Schjerfbeck · 1915 · oil on canvas

I carry the world on my back,
a cup and flask to drink, bread
that will not weight me.
I carry the clear Finnish light
to save its summer flame.

I dispose of what I can until
the face is plainly empty, till
I behold the road, its fork,
the small steps tread.
I set cornerstones to anchor

paint to more than earth, even if
at times it is myself.

I remove details like brush
cleared from the spruce forest.
Study my face as if stranger—
cleft of chin, salmon cheeks,
cloudberry lips, pale skin.

Background dark-dark-dark
like the infinite winter night.
At the edge of Helsinki Harbour,
I set down the world. I rinse
my visage in the Baltic Sea.

Electric Prisms

Sonia Delaunay · 1914 · oil on canvas

Black locusts on the Boulevard
stitch branches, thick embroidery
on linen clouds as we stroll

arm-in-arm across the park,
dusk dimming everything
till even we are gone.

And then—the prismatic flash—
a string of new street lamplights
that cast aside the stars.

Electricity.

What luminosity, you say.

As for myself—it pierced a pinhole
in my heart, bled a strange elation,
though that night I could not

comprehend this new god nor know
how it would slowly kill the dark—

keep us awake at night, encircling.

The Fortune Teller

Suzanne Valadon • 1912 • oil on canvas

After years spent modeling, I know how
it feels to lie naked for hours, the seconds
unfolding as slowly as a flower blooms.
Skin goose-bumped by the slightest breeze
traveling across the artist's open studio.
I have brushed this knowledge into
the painting, creating a twist on the *odalisque*—
not slave nor prostitute, but one determined
to control the ending. Strong lines, ample weight,
reclined on right elbow and hip, cool as chilled milk.
Nude to better absorb. I have cut the composition
horizontally—body on settee, the soothsayer set
on the carpet below as she reads the circle of cards.
Seer holds the queen of diamonds in her hand.

Self-Portrait on the Sixth Wedding Anniversary

Paula Modersohn-Becker · 1906 · tempera on canvas

Did you leave some Thing behind, some
place that cannot bear your absence

—Rainer Maria Rilke, "Requiem for a Friend"

How can it be only months ago you painted this self-portrait
while pregnant? The amber necklace hanging
round your neck and breasts, the opal
sheet slung low across your hips—
it seems a sacrificial cloth, as if
you could see the future.

Eighteen days after childbirth, you will stand
again in this room
black blood trickling down pale legs,
viscous as egg.
Eighteen days a mother
with a daughter
and barely thirty, now reeling
from the embolism of a ruptured life.

We stand before the door and fear
that you are leaving—

Your dear friend Rilke knew you did not want
to be a wife. Did you want to be a mother?

We enter. The wallpapered room collecting dust,
the flax-light fading.

You stare at us with those almond eyes
as if you held some secret. Quiet
so we might hear the first words
of Rilke's requiem for your soul—

I have my dead and I have let them go

Sita and Sarita

Cecilia Beaux • 1893–94 • oil on canvas

To my dear sister Etta,

Of cherished childhood days, the ones
that cling—you sitting with me as I sketch
in the walled garden, teacakes and lemonade
set out under the linden—small comforts
for loneliness. Stones pillowed with moss,
brambled roses protecting us, the green
garden gate with its small latch that clicked
like teeth when we closed it.

Us missing mama, who spent only
twelve short days on this earth once I
was born. And papa who left us with his
sorrow. Perhaps I seek solace in portraiture,
a way to grasp a glimpse of both. Since *Sita
and Sarita* is commissioned work, I have decided
to paint a copy for myself. Sarita reminds me
of you, the wistful gaze we both know too well.

Last night I dreamed I could see the future—
First Lady Eleanor Roosevelt laying her hand
upon my shoulder, recognizing my contributions
to American art and culture. When I awoke,
Sita and Sarita—still on the easel—implored
me to finish the work. I looked outside
at the passing clouds and could see
mama nodding her approval.

With abiding love,

Leilie

THE MAID IN THE KITCHEN

Anna Ancher • 1883–6 • oil on canvas

We were spending two days in Copenhagen
and I knew she was here.
Thought she was at the Statens Museum
but I didn't see her. Asked a docent

who said, *she's at the Hirschsprung.*
It was 3:30, the doors would close at 4:00.

I hurried down a path through the park
and arrived with minutes to spare,
paid the fee of ten Krone
and rushed
towards the interior door
and even from there

I could see her in the kitchen,
the first painting on the far wall.

A door ajar lets in a rib of light—

she faces away from us
cutting-peeling-washing something
green, there's a small white bag
something blue, a soft rag,
she's wearing a long, red skirt
a shirt dark as charcoal, she's in shadow
the half-curtain in front of her
closed, is luminous.

Why doesn't she open it?

The Umbrella

Marie Bashkirtseff · 1883 · oil on canvas

TB like a felt coat
inside a lung
a last day
when she will wake
and paint herself
the forecast:
clouds with rain.

She leaves her diary.

Grips the black
umbrella, repellent
as a crow's back,
its thin ribs expanded
in particular places
to support
the canopy, fixed
to the delicate joints
like fine bones.

It fills the frame—

as if Death refuses to wait,
has brought
the piceous garments
of cloak and gloves
to the girl
with the palest face.

Sunshine in the Blue Room

Anna Ancher • 1891 • oil on canvas • plus six more paintings by the artist

Sunshine in the blind woman's room.
Young girl before a lamp.
Interior with chair and plant.
Interior with sunlight and red door.
Young girl arranging flowers.
a funeral.

Gallery IV

Paintings 1878 – 1559

Moonlight, study

Fanny Churberg · 1878 · oil on canvas

She has brought her luminous self
viscous as white glue to this place,
the clouds filling with moon-milk

she has called the night things
out of lamp black, an outburst—

Churberg's brushstrokes are like van Gogh's
(though she came before him)

put down her brushes just as he was starting
(both painted for ten short years)

neither knew the other, the way
they both shattered things in color—

rock, tundra, tree, feverish flowers.

She churns Nordic moonlight like butter
her fingerprints of frenzied clouds backlit,

the foreground sloped and scrubbed
with a furious brush, the black silhouette
of two houses—

one watching with a yellow eye.

A Nun

Henriette Browne · 1859 · oil on canvas

The time of day set still as stone for prayer
Nones, that ninth hour after dawn, that place
I'm looking, the wimple framing her young face
Drawn to shadow under chin, the sheer black habit
Of praying, the pages with their red rims.
The long path on the way to finding grace.
Her heavy lids like louvers closing in
On infinity. She seems a novice—
A cover girl for nuns—the parchment robe,
Small missal. A unity within the whole.
The composition perfectly triangulated
Each shape both solid and weightless
The invisible visible. Something pellucid I remember
Kneeling in a pew—nave, nun, pale light.

Ploughing in the Nivernais

Rosa Bonheur • 1849 • oil on canvas

October 18, 1849
Feast Day of Saint Luke
Patron Saint of Oxen and Artists

Dear Saint Luke,

Today, my thoughts are with you and our
beloved oxen. I remember my vision at age eleven
when sick with scarlet fever, I heard you call
from heaven, and what appeared did cure me—
an ox draped in gold raiment, my devotion
sealed at that moment. And father bless him,
brought home a menagerie, allowing them
to freely wander through the house. Each day
I pray, believing there is no difference between
us animals, though some will feign it.

In honor of your feast day, I have finally
finished the painting, given the oxen a final coat
of cream and chestnut as they plough the earth
and lead the men. When I depart from this world
I pray an ox like one of these will lead me on
the journey. Last night as I cleaned my brushes,
a stag stood outside the window listening to
the wind. His presence reminded me to write
to you this morning.

Know I will always remain your humble
servant. Any recognition for my work will never
match the feeling that overcomes me as I walk
in the forest here in Fontainebleau and time opens
into its infiniteness as I sketch the flanks of the great
oxen and smell their heat. I kneel before you as artist
and animal, one and the same, until my numbered
days shall pass like summer rain. Then take me as I am.

Forever in faith,

Rosa

Self-Portrait Hesitating between Music and Painting

Angelica Kauffman • 1794 • oil on canvas

She is caught in the moment between two Muses—
Music, in her vermilion dress on the viewer's left,
and Painting dressed in brilliant blue on her right.
She's holding Music's hand but has an open one
and she is leaning, the heroine in her own tug of war
that *in between* feeling—you know the one—pulling
both ends of a rope and afraid of being burned.
She knows the story of Hercules, the hero wrestling
virtue and pleasure before choosing his destiny, but wants
an answer of her own. Where would we be without
our myths and history? Music with her sheet of song
and scores, Painting with her palette and brushes—
Who will be the strongest, who will she love more?
For what they are but also for what else they are.

Self-Portrait

Elisabeth Vigée Le Brun · 1790 · oil on canvas

After all those years painting patron Marie Antoinette
and her royal court, all those diamond pebbles
and blue veins throbbing under sweating temples
before the Queen's beheading—here the artist's mindset

turns to *I*, a mirrored gaze, some gauzed muslin
wrapped around her head of curls, not to obscure
but—*to know thyself*—inside the contours
of the body, subject and object becoming one.

How do we ever know when the work is done?
Palette and brushes clutched in her left hand,
she brushes in a final stroke to understand
herself—absorbed like water taken by a sponge.

METAMORPHOSIS

Maria Sibylla Merian • 1705 • Plate 18: Spiders, ants and hummingbird on a branch of guava

Between the seen and the imagined
it was the silkworms I loved first,
the egg hatch and larvae squirm
before the smooth cocoon, the open door—
wings drying on the floor of a mulberry leaf.

A thousand years ago in Frankfurt
I reared my caterpillars and two daughters
for twenty years and watched them
grow inch-by-inch until
they were born again as butterflies.

At fifty-two, I sold my drawings to pay
my way, sailing south to Surinam,
a middle-aged woman in an old age
searching for survival in the hothouse
of Eden, miraculous spiracles of breathing.

I sketched insects and plants in rainforests,
gardens, the jungled shores near Paramaribo.
I tore my petticoat. My stockings. I climbed
the branches and collected, filling my folio until
I fell sick and sailed home to compose my opus—

Metamorphosis Insectorum Surinamensium.
Come closer to this painting in my hands—
the cold cockroach with her buzzing lantern
flies, the tarantula devouring the remains
of a hollow hummingbird.

Flowers in a Glass Vase

Rachel Ruysch · 1704 · oil on canvas

Again, flowers are posing for portraits—
the glass vase firmly placed
        open for holding
waiting for an audience of anyone

the cast is the artist's choosing
this one, that one—
        convolvulus, ranunculus
morning glory, red trumpet, cabbage rose

bugs and beetles are flying in
their faces   they're also viewers
and everyone too soon   will be gone
the gatherer   and gathered

you don't need to know
there are ten children pulling on her petticoat
hundreds of portraits   still to paint
at some point   legs give out

rootless stems bend   the backdrop
dark as molasses

some seconds left of vanitas
then viscous clouds of water
ruthless   as another rots

Still Life of Flowers

Rachel Ruysch · 1708 · oil on canvas · plus
twelve more paintings by the artist

Flowerpiece with prunes.
Roses, tulips, ranunculus and other
flowers in a glass vase, with plums. Spray of flowers
with insects and butterflies on a marble slab. Posy of
flowers, with a red admiral butterfly, on a marble ledge.
Flowers, fruit, reptiles, and insects on the edge of a wood.
Still life of fruits, animals and insects on a moss floor.
Spray of flowers, with a beetle on a stone balustrade.
Flowers in a glass vase with a cricket in a niche . . .
with peaches and red berries, on a marble slab.
with insects and peaches, on a marble
tabletop. with pomegranates
on a marble balustrade.
on a balustrade
with colonnade.

The Triumph of Bacchus

Michaelina Wautier • c. 1659 • oil on canvas

Dear Viewer,

A curator found the painting in a closet
in Vienna after several centuries, cleaned it
to properly present to you, the people.
I painted the bacchanal larger than life
and included a dozen male nudes, two
hundred years before women were allowed to.
I even disguised myself as one of the revelers
but I think you can tell it is me. I have exposed
my left breast and I am the only one brave
enough to face you.
I know we must always be ready to be
discovered, but it is difficult to not despair.
Time has only so many hands. So many ticks.
What short triumph our Roman friend
Bacchus was allowed, the last green grapes
divided among the cherubs and the little men.
God of wine, son of Zeus, I do not think
he saw it coming. Devouring the fermented
fruit as if it were his last meal, and all of them
too fooled by wine, the sin of too much
comfort, its false elation.
Who can envision the final scene
of any one life? The days cut and crushed
then poured into a chalice to sip, then sleep.
To live again a distant dream.

From an earlier century,

Michaelina Wautier

Judith Slaying Holofernes

Artemisa Gentileschi • 1611–12 • oil on canvas

Let us walk down the hall to the murder scene
with our heroines—Judith and Abra—to the bedchamber
where Holofernes lies stretched across the mattress,
chiaroscuro controlling the biblical story.

The artist has brought his blood to the foreground
so we might smell its sticky sweetness, better see
the rivulets streaking the creased bedsheets,
weigh who tips the scales: forgiveness or revenge.

Judith wears a royal blue gown to mark the occasion—
dabs of pigment push her sleeves up muscular arms.
Her left hand presses firmly against his head, her
right hand grips the cross-shaped sword.

The maidservant Abra assists the widow's hand—
both braced against the frame until the work is done.
Have you ever held a kitchen knife and thought
how some light might save you?

Noli Me Tangere

Lavinia Fontana · 1581 · oil on canvas

In her depiction of the Resurrection
Jesus stands barefoot with his spade in the garden

Mary Magdalene crouches
her saffron robe creased in shadow
she's wearing sandals

and there's that split second
when she realizes who
he is, he says:
        don't touch me

he's wearing a straw hat instead of the halo
and holds the spade but is not ready
to dig in

the middle distance holds a muted light
the tomb empty   and Mary?

maybe she smells the dirt of fear
the black crumbs of sour bread,
wants to touch the wounds for proof

or wants to pinch her own flesh to test
whether she is the invisible one

though here she wears the halo,
holds the scepter, knows
every body leaves a womb—

Bernandino Campi Painting Sofonisba Anguissola

Sofonisba Anguissola · 1559 · oil on canvas

I, Sofonisba Anguissola, stand before you—
painting my former teacher painting me, the girl
who once drew a crayfish-bitten boy so well
I made him cry, drawing the praise of Michelangelo.

I have given the man a silver mahlstick to steady
the hand that holds the brush as he paints
the bodice of my red-madder dress. No mistake,
it's more a dare—a double portrait I'm controlling—

knowing just where to set my gaze to pierce the space
so I am free to leave the frame and join you, the viewer.
I have made Campi no old master, myself no apprentice.
I, Sofonisba Anguissola, stand at my easel in a dark time

mixing pigments for my own skin. Have lit a fire
with a three-way mirror so you can more clearly see—
be drawn in to close attention— not to the beauty
of a person or thing, but to its apprehension.

The Closing
Fourteen Paintings by Mary Frank

This is the remembering (open).

What color lament?

Knowing by heart (open).
Migration (open).

Knowing by heart (closed).
Migration (closed).

Where or when? (open)

Ballad (open).
Creature and ruins.
Ballad (closed).

Did you ever?
Reach.
Destinies.

This is the remembering (closed).

Artists

Artist	*Birthplace*	*Years Lived*
Sofonisba Anguissola	Cremona, Italy	c. 1532–1625
Lavinia Fontana	Bologna, Italy	1552–1614
Artemisa Gentileschi	Rome, Italy	1593–1653
Michaelina Wautier	Mons, Belgium	c. 1604–1689
Maria Sibylla Merian	Frankfurt, Germany	1647–1717
Rachel Ruysch	The Hague, Netherlands	1664–1750
Angelica Kauffman	Chur, Switzerland	1741–1807
Elisabeth Vigée Le Brun	Paris, France	1755–1842
Rosa Bonheur	Bordeaux, France	1822–1899
Henriette Browne	Paris, France	1829–1901
Fanny Churberg	Vaasa, Finland	1845–1892
Cecilia Beaux	Philadelphia, Pa., USA	1855–1942
Marie Bashkirtseff	Havrontsi, Ukraine	1858–1884
Anna Ancher	Skagen, Denmark	1859–1935
Helene Schjerfbeck	Helsinki, Finland	1862–1946
Suzanne Valadon	Bessines-sur-Gartempe, France	1865–1938
Paula Modersohn-Becker	Dresden, Germany	1876–1907
Sonia Delaunay	Gradiesk, Ukraine	1885–1979
Tarsila do Amaral	Capivari, Brazil	1886–1973
Ida Ten Eyck O'Keeffe	Sun Prairie, Wis., USA	1889–1961
Dorrit Black	Adelaide, Australia	1891–1951
Alma Thomas	Columbus, Ga., USA	1891–1978
Dod Procter	London, UK	1890–1972
Amelia Peláez	Yaguajay, Cuba	1896–1968
Kay Sage	Watervliet, N.Y., USA	1898–1963
Frida Kahlo	Coyoacán, Mexico	1907–1954
Lee Krasner	New York City, N.Y., USA	1908–1984
Helen Lundeberg	Chicago, Ill., USA	1908–1999
Rita Angus	Hastings, New Zealand	1908–1970
Agnes Martin	Macklin, Canada	1912–2004
Ángeles Santos	Portbou, Spain	1911–2013
Natalia Dumitrescu	Bucharest, Romania	1915–1997

Artist	*Birthplace*	*Years Lived*
Sandra Blow	London, UK	1925–2006
Etel Adnan	Beirut, Lebanon	1925–
Tilsa Tsuchiya	Supe, Peru	1932–1984
Mary Frank	London, UK	1933–
Joan Brown	San Francisco, Calif., USA	1938–1999
Vija Celmins	Riga, Latvia	1938–
Jennifer Bartlett	Long Beach, Calif., USA	1941–
Astrid Preston	Stockholm, Sweden	1945–
Lucy Mackenzie	Sudan	1952–
April Gornick	Cleveland, Ohio, USA	1953–
Karen Kitchel	Battlecreek, Mich., USA	1957–
Emmi Whitehorse	Crownpoint, N.M., USA	1957–
Tina Mion	Washington, D.C., USA	1960–
Julie Mehretu	Addis Ababa, Ethiopia	1970–
Amy Sherald	Columbus, Ga., USA	1973–

Notes

The title is borrowed from the Greek word *Chroma*, meaning color.

The collection is inspired by the paintings of forty-seven women artists working over five centuries and born in twenty-five different countries. Some were well known within their circles and times, others worked in relative obscurity. The youngest died at twenty-five, the oldest at 101; some are painting at this very moment.

The "exhibition" is arranged in four "galleries" presented in reverse chronological order, taking the viewer/reader into the past and the history of art as seen through paintings by women artists.

The galleries include six "painting title" or "found" poems—"Box of Coloured Objects," "Night Flying In," "Postcard," "Sunshine in the Blue Room," Still Life of Flowers," and "Fourteen Paintings by Mary Frank"—created using a selection of painting titles from the noted artists. The periods within the poems indicate breaks between painting titles. The only poem title of the six that is not a painting is "Fourteen Paintings by Mary Frank."

Poem titles reference the title of the art piece that is the inspiration for the poem. Each poem's epigraph lists the name of the artist as well as the piece's date and medium, just as you would find in curator's notes in a museum or gallery.

Most paintings dated before 1920 may be found on Wikimedia Commons. If not there, a search for the painting can direct the reader to the museum where the artwork is located. The more modern pieces may also be found on the artist's website or a linked gallery website.

[13] The opening poem, "Fourteen Ways of Looking at a Painting," was inspired by "Thirteen Ways of Looking at a Blackbird" by Wallace Stevens.

[23] The observation by Vija Celmins in "Ocean" is from the *TateShots* video interview "Painting Takes Just a Second to Go In."

[27] The year after I first viewed Amy Sherald's award-winning painting "Miss Everything (Unsuppressed Deliverance)" at the Smithsonian National Portrait Gallery, First Lady Michelle Obama chose Sherald to paint her official First Lady portrait.

[29] "Mount Tamalpais" is a found poem using seventy-six words from Etel Adnan's essay *Journey to Mount Tamalpais* (Sausalito: The Post-Apollo Press, 1986).

[35] The quote by Alma Thomas is from *Alma W. Thomas: A Retrospective of the Paintings,* an exhibition catalog for the show organized by the Fort Wayne Museum of Art in 1998.

Acknowledgments

Grateful acknowledgment is made to the editors of the following journals in which these poems, or versions of these poems, first appeared:

Ekphrasis: "Metamorphosis" and "Self-Portrait on the Sixth Wedding Anniversary"

The Ekphrastic Review: "I Have No Shadow," "Judith Slaying Holofernes," "A Nun," "On Me Fait Signe," and "Self-Portrait with Black Background"

FORTH: "Un Mundo"

LIGHT-A Journal of Photography and Poetry: "Self-Portrait Hesitating Between Music and Painting"

Silkworm 13: "Empirical Construction, Istanbul" and "The Fortune Teller"

SPANK the CARP: "A Flower Poem in Two Parts" ("Flowers in a Glass Vase" and "Still Life of Flowers")

SWWIM: "Air: 24 Hours, Five P.M."

Voice of Eve: "Self-Portrait" and "Fishes"

Thanks also to the Northampton Arts Council for selecting "Morning Glory" as part of the *2019 Visual Arts and Poetry Biennial: From Seed to Fruition*

Many thanks to the women artists who created the paintings that inspired these poems. Special thanks to Jean Blakeman, Libby Maxey, Rebecca Hart Olander, and Adin Thayer for Wednesday poetry nights and for being there for the journey. Also thanks to Beth Filson and the Thursday night writing group. To my friends and family, my deepest gratitude. I am always thankful to my greatest loves: my husband, John Hird, and our children, Kelly, William, and Samuel. Thank you for believing in me and in the power of art.

About the Author

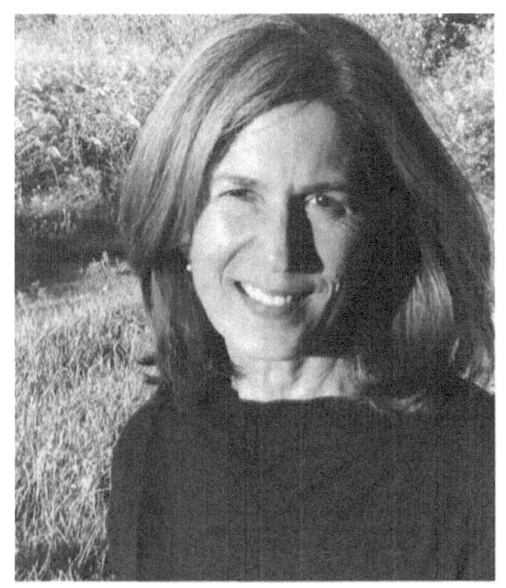

Sharon Tracey is a writer and editor, and author of the poetry collection *What I Remember Most Is Everything* (All Caps Publishing, 2017). Her poems have appeared in *The Worcester Review, Mom Egg Review, Tule Review,* and *The Ekphrastic Review,* among others. Art and nature are recurring themes in her work, and art and painting have been lifelong passions. Prior to returning to writing full-time, she worked at the University of Massachusetts Amherst as a director of environmental programs and later as a communications director. She holds a Master's degree from the University of California, Berkeley and lives in western Massachusetts.

www.ingramcontent.com/pod-product-compliance
Lightning Source LLC
LaVergne TN
LVHW051016080826
845145LV00009B/2655

* 9 7 8 1 9 5 1 6 5 1 4 9 7 *